A fashionable children's tale for grown-ups

DAVID LONGSHAW

For Kirsty

DAVID LONGSHAW
PRESENTS TO YOU,
MAUDE & DORIS
THE STORY OF MILDRED
(A fashionable children's tale for grown-ups.)
Written and illustrated by David Longshaw.

First E published in Great Britain 2014
Text and illustrations copyright David Longshaw 2014
David Longshaw Ltd

To see more of David's work – including fashion design, illustration and animation – go to:

WWW.DAVIDLONGSHAW.CO.UK

MILDRED

To see more of David's work — including fashion design, illustration and animation — go to:

www.davidlongshaw.co.uk

DAVID LONGSHAW

INTRODUCES

MAUDE

PERTINENCE

MILDRED

FOUL MOUTHED HOUSE
MOUSE

DORIS

THE PERCIES

To see more of David's work – including fashion design, illustration and animation – go to:

WWW.davidlongshaw.co.uk

Ooh, you are a peculiar one, you. What are you up to now?

I asked in an, 'I'm not sure I want to hear the answer' sort of a voice.

Replied Mildred (dressed in Kirsty Ward) in a tone to suggest that this was a perfectly normal way to do things.

I debated with myself whether to enquire how exactly sticking the magazine on her head was going to help her absorb any sort of information

(dressed as I was in David Longshaw).

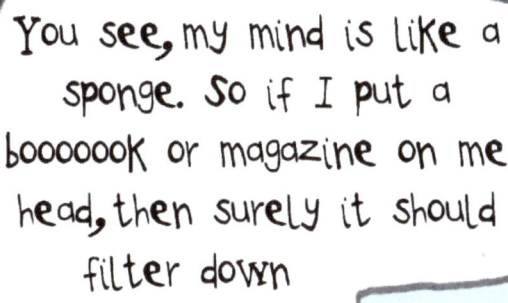

You see, my mind is like a sponge. So if I put a boooooook or magazine on me head, then surely it should filter down

continued Mildred after a time.

Right... You do know it doesn't work like that? The words and the pictures aren't going to just filter into your head.

"Aren't they? Well, why ever not? They should do, you knoooow, it makes sense, dunt it?." she replied dejectedly.

"Well not really. You have to see the pages and read the words for your mind to take in the information," I said despairingly.

How curious. Well I suppose I should take it off my head then

the peculiar little penguin said disappointedly. She sat for a while next to me not saying much.

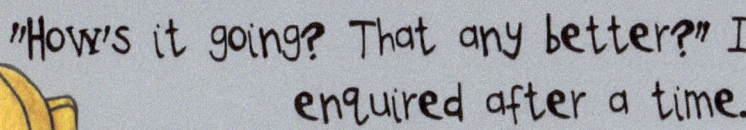

"How's it going? That any better?" I enquired after a time.

Yes, thank you, much.

said Mildred in a rather short tone. "What are you looking at?" I asked simply enough, peering over to have a look at the page she had been gazing at for the last half an hour.

"Do you mind? I'm trying to concentrate. It's private,"

she said moodily as she clambered down from her stool,

standing the magazine on it and burying her head in the pages, so I couldn't see.

7

"Fair enough," I replied, a little confused, as it was my magazine (MAUDEZINE, the whole magazine is about me!).

About ten minutes later she poked her little head up and said, "Do you know, I've been staring at this magazine for ages and I've not managed to absorb anything other than this page? I'm not too sure your method works."

"Well, if you don't look at any other pages, you're not going to be able to absorb any more, are you?" I replied.

"You mean, I have to turn the pages and loooooook at each one individual like. Ooh, that's too much effort for me. Sod this, I'm off to watch TV, they move the images for you on that."

And off she popped.

8

This is the story of a
curious creature called
Mildred, who lives in
a dress.

The passage you've just read was a typical
encounter with Mildred, the peculiar penguin
who has enriched, complicated and confused our
lives from our very first encounter to the
present day.

I met Mildred through a good
friend of mine, the Foul
Mouthed House Mouse.

I'm Maude, by the way.
For those of you (the
small minority) who are

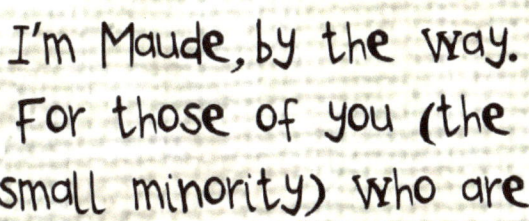

ignorant and
unaware of me
and my vast
influence,

I am Editor-in-Chief of
Maudezine,

the highly influential fashion bible.
I have appeared in everything
from VOGUE to LOVE magazine,
to the cover of the London
Fashion Week's newspaper and
even the famous
Saint Martins' catwalk.

10

I'm a sort of fabric mouse (by sort of, I mean other than my colour and I suppose if you squint, my head and ears, I look sod all like a mouse, having scaled down human proportions as I do).
I measure 32cm in height and am made from 100% cashmere

(the finest quality available I'll have you know).
But I'm sure you already knew all of that.

Mildred is now Maudezine's resident agony aunt and is (most of the time when she's not getting over excited and forgetting herself) a valuable member of the editorial team. She's even appeared in a number of publications herself (obviously not as many as I have).

But back to the story and how Mildred became the influential Maudezinest you all know and love. Mildred stumbled in to our lives, as I said, through a chance meeting with the Foul Mouthed House Mouse (such a wonderful creature, but as her name suggests she is a tad potty mouthed).

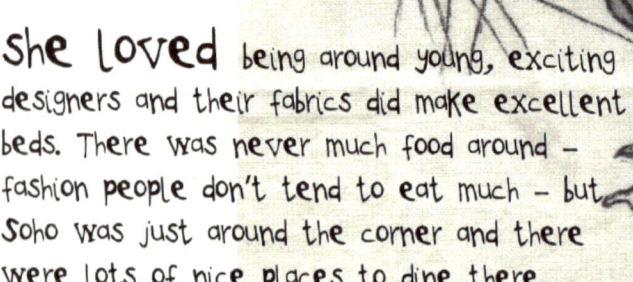

The Foul mouthed House Mouse

had popped in to one of the lockers in the fashion department at Saint Martins (this was back in the days when it was on Charring Cross Road, London) where she was living;

she loved being around young, exciting designers and their fabrics did make excellent beds. There was never much food around — fashion people don't tend to eat much — but Soho was just around the corner and there were lots of nice places to dine there.

The Foul Mouthed House mouse was just getting comfortable and nestling down in some sheepskin when suddenly she heard what sounded like a bizarre northern accent with a speech impediment.

Who the !*&* is that?

she said as she
looked around.

"Heloooooooo! My naaaaaam's
Mildred! I'm obsessed! You see I know
the TRUTH!
In all of us there is a certain **percentage**,
which is **pure dress!** I know this sounds
strange but it's true. But the problem is, you
see, my clothes aren't conveying the true dress
in me, they simply don't correlate!"

14

'I see.' said the Foul Mouthed House Mouse as she spotted the small penguin who had just approached her from behind.

'But do you? You know, that is to say, by wearing and being in an environment with clothing,

we actually take on their characteristics, their style, our persona is intricately woooven into the character

of our dress and therefore the character we project as people, or in my case a peculiarly small penguin," continued Mildred machinegun like.

15

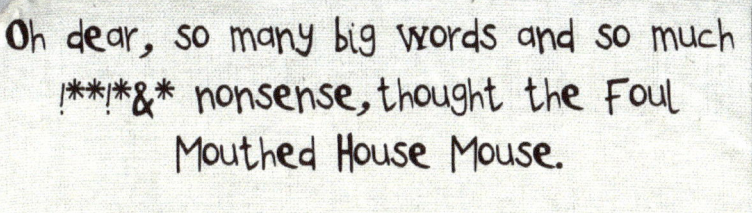

Oh dear, so many big words and so much !**!*&* nonsense, thought the Foul Mouthed House Mouse.

Despite her obsession with clothing, though, I'm afraid to say that Mildred had never found her sense of style.

"I love your dress. Werd ya get it from?

Oooooh, I just knoow it says so much about ya. It just wreaks sophistication, edginess. OOOOh I luve it. It's so avant-garde; it's so now, but ultimately timeless. Where'd ya get it?

Ooh, where'd ya get it? I love it! I wan one! Oh, can I ave it! No, I must get me ooown. Oh, I love it! I need somein like that. But different, ya nooooo. Yeh YEH, me own version."

17

The conversation, if you can call it that—probably Mildred monologue is a more apt description—

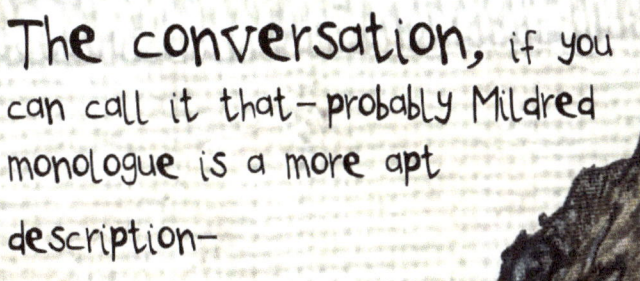

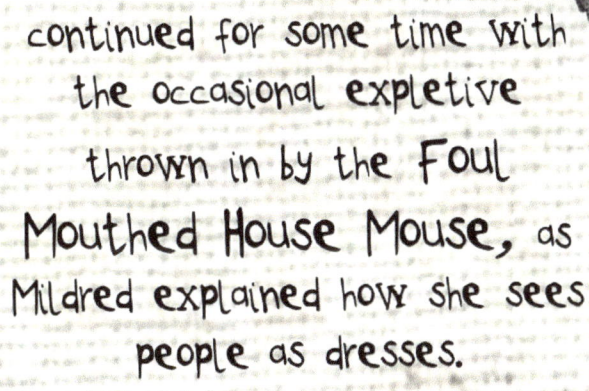

continued for some time with the occasional expletive thrown in by the Foul Mouthed House Mouse, as Mildred explained how she sees people as dresses.

The Foul Mouthed House Mouse was a tad surprised/ disturbed by Mildred, especially by her theories about people and animals being part dress.

But she was also intrigued and thought **Mildred** to be an interesting penguin, so decided to try to help her **find her true self through the medium of clothing.**

You could say it's almost like Dorothy in 'The Wizard of Oz', trying to find a heart for the Scarecrow, or the Tin Man, or whichever one it was.

But how was **Mildred's** style to be **found?**

Oh strange, strange little thing that she was

Oh strange, strange little thing that she was, The **Foul Mouthed House Mouse** felt that she suited her own apparel quite well. It had its roots in Savile Row tailoring (through fabrication), fused with the urban wear she knew and loved (which is intriguing, as Foul Mouthed House Mouse came from a cottage in the countryside and is a mouse, so has never worn clothes until now, but let's not split hairs) with its air of casualness and mandatory hood, partly for style and comfort, partly because hoodies were such a political issue at the time of design, the wearing of them being banned from certain shopping malls, etc. **Mildred** too felt some affinity with the urban uniform of the street, but yet her

sensitivities were different from that of the

Foul Mouthed House Mouse and though

she loved a bit of **Savile Row** tailoring, "Ooh, it's wonderful!", it just wasn't very her. Mildred was more feminine. She was a delicate soul, she saw people as dresses, she was not as brash as the Foul Mouthed House Mouse. If she had to be described as a colour, she was more pink than grey, more floral pattern than pinstripe, but this didn't fully cover her unique personality. She wanted more than just a floral dress, more than frills and pink bows.

20

Being a **peculiar shape** and size and of course, a penguin, **Mildred** had found it hard to find dresses to wear in the first place, so had become quite skilled at making her own.

Unfortunately, her abilities as a **designer** had if anything regressed from what was a pretty rubbish starting point. So the results, as you can imagine, were, erm, **interesting to be polite.**

Perhaps we need to go into Mildred's past to throw some light on her dilemma. As you may have noticed, Mildred was sensitive, so sensitive in fact that she felt she should share her empathy for suffering with others.

She had trained at the local college (which prided itself on running short courses for just about everything) as a counsellor. And even though you couldn't really see Mildred's ears, she was a very, very good listener. Misery was her forte; misery through poor dress sense her speciality.

But no matter how many magazines she read and celebs she studied, she couldn't get the hang of wearing clothes that suited her.

Her confidence as a professional was non-existent. How could she fill others with hope or offer advice about shoes, dresses or accessories if she looked like a bag of washing?

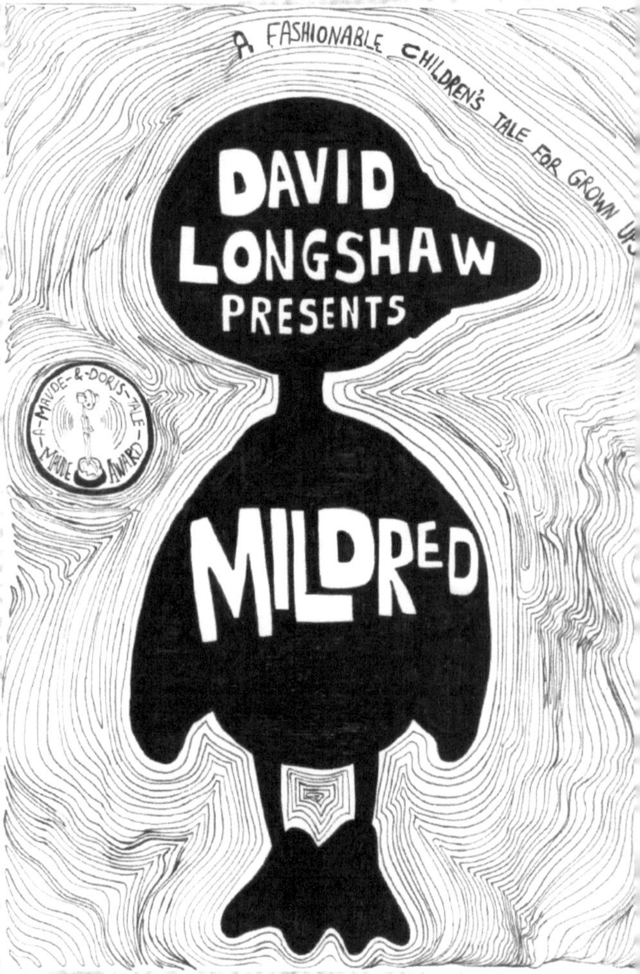

The Foul Mouthed House Mouse understood how she felt. She had been

A FASHIONABLE CHILDREN'S TALE FOR GROWN UPS

DAVID LONGSHAW PRESENTS

MILDRED

A MAUDE & DORIS TALE MAUDE AWARD

23

lucky that she knew me (Maude) and that I had been able to help her find her own style. So once more it was to me she came to seek advice, (I was sharing a cake with boozy Doris at the time).

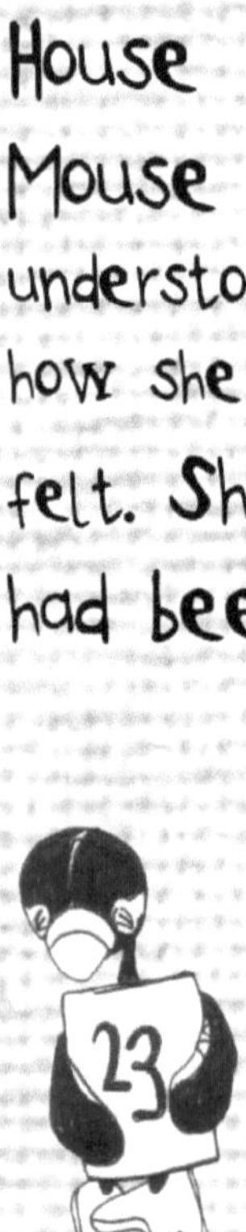

When I met Mildred, I immediately understood her plight, so I introduced her to some designer friends of mine who promised to help.

However, the problem with fashion designers—in fact most designers, be it of cutlery, bedding or film sets—is that they tend to follow their **artistic vision** rather than what is necessarily the best look for their client.

24

The first designer Mildred went to wanted her to look like a Grecian goddess.

The **second** created a piece (a dress to the likes of you) that made **Mildred** look like some elaborate fairy who wouldn't look out of place on top of a cake or Christmas tree.

26

Mildred was too individual for this, she felt restricted by the excessive femininity of it all. The Foul Mouthed House Mouse agreed as she shouted,

"That's !*&*$*% hilarious, that is!" and chuckled at the frothy pink creation.

The next designer was very into
theatrical, statement pieces

(clothes to you) and
exaggerated millinery
(that's hats to you) .

29

Though **Mildred** thought the creations were wonderful, they just didn't feel right, she didn't want to stand out too overtly.

No, they were **beautiful** but were more suited to the catwalk than her everyday life.

The penultimate designer I took Mildred to was very into 'shapes',

meaning everything had a slightly angular look.

31

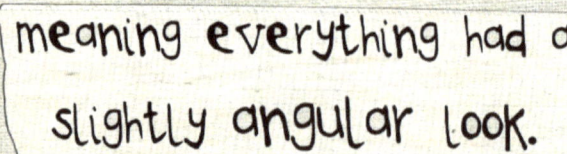

She also liked the Foul Mouthed
House Mouse's hoody,
so made a version of it in pink for
Mildred,
which was a bit cheeky as it was another
design original creation. But despite this
plagiarism, still nothing suited
Mildred's needs, wants or desires.

32

Mildred was even sadder than before.

I felt absolutely awful. The process of
finding Mildred's personality in dress form had

been an unmitigated disaster.

33

I considered asking for help from my good friends at Dior, Givenchy, Prada or even Karl at Chanel, but the gravity of the situation required not only an unparalleled designer and fashion genius, but also someone who could empathise

with the plight of this **peculiar** fabric **penguin.**

I myself had fought (and won) my
battles with the fashion industry and a
world at large that was just not ready

for a fabric fashion force such as myself.
So I decided the only course of action to
be taken was for me (Maude) to create
a wondrous wardrobe for Mildred myself
(that's lots of clothes to you).

I got cracking in a whirl of activity with the help of my trusty sidekick, boozy Doris and a plethora of Percies bouncing around, doing whatever was asked of them (well, most of the time).

36

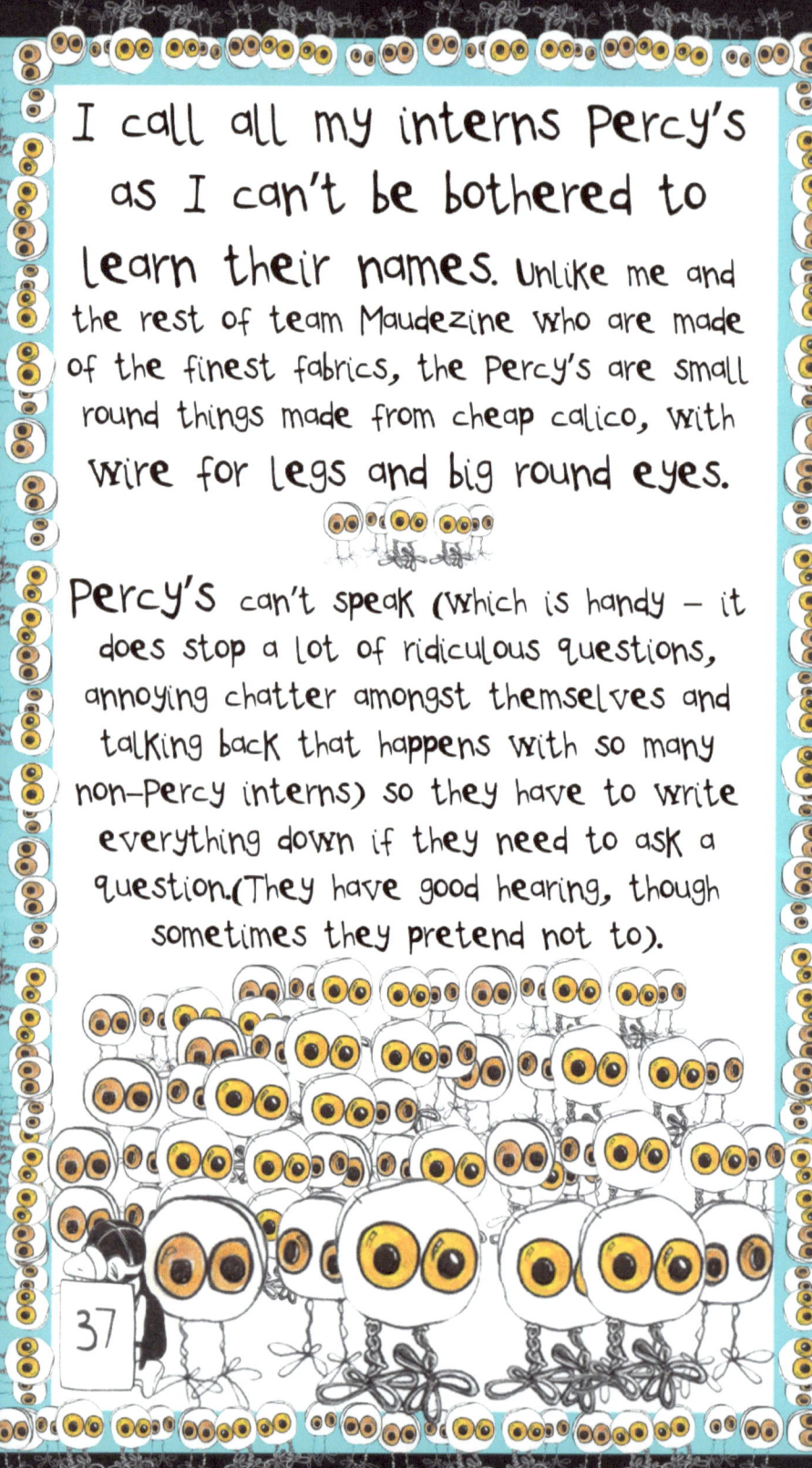

I call all my interns Percy's as I can't be bothered to learn their names. Unlike me and the rest of team Maudezine who are made of the finest fabrics, the Percy's are small round things made from cheap calico, with wire for legs and big round eyes.

Percy's can't speak (which is handy — it does stop a lot of ridiculous questions, annoying chatter amongst themselves and talking back that happens with so many non-Percy interns) so they have to write everything down if they need to ask a question.(They have good hearing, though sometimes they pretend not to).

37

Me (Maude) and Doris busy working hard.

Designs were scribbled, fabrics chosen and woven especially for us by the best mills in England, Scotland and Italy. Patterns drafted, toiles made (that's prototypes to the likes of you). The sewing machines and Peries worked through the night and even the Foul Mouthed House Mouse tried to lend a hand cutting out the fabrics and sewing.

I didn't work throughout the night, of course. I had far too many fashion parties to attend and beauty sleep to be had – which is its own type of work, this kind of Maudnificence doesn't just happen, you know?

39

After many days and hours of toil a whole range of amazing apparel appeared (that's clothes to you).

I had created all manner of **Maudaliciously** spectacular pieces for Mildred to wear (again, that's clothes to you) for every occasion - from not so casual daywear to not so casual weekend wear. It was trans-seasonal in a non-trans-seasonal directional, yet bang on trend, yet not being a slave to trends style and in many ways transcending trends.

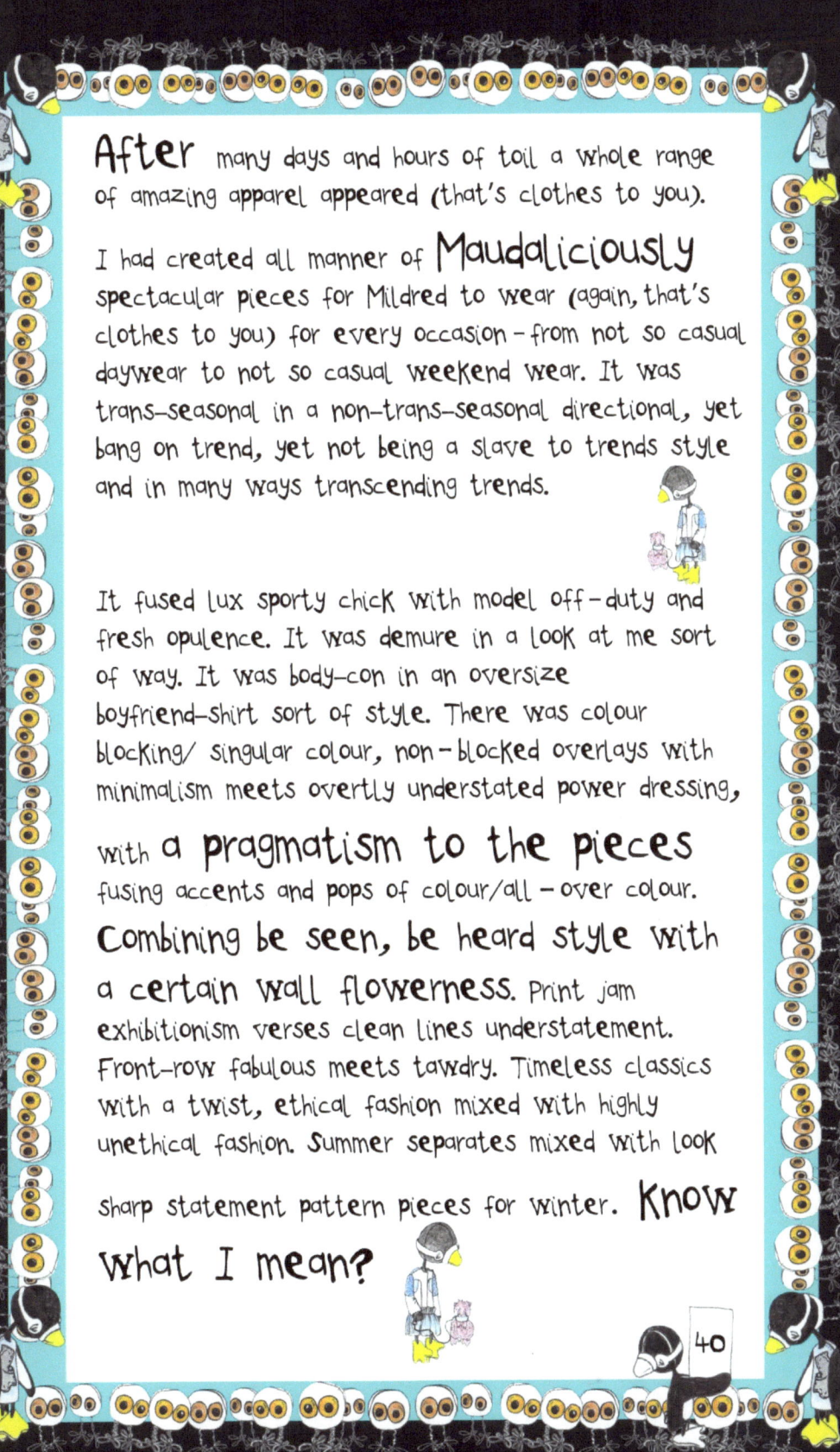

It fused lux sporty chick with model off-duty and fresh opulence. It was demure in a look at me sort of way. It was body-con in an oversize boyfriend-shirt sort of style. There was colour blocking/ singular colour, non-blocked overlays with minimalism meets overtly understated power dressing,

with **a pragmatism to the pieces** fusing accents and pops of colour/all-over colour. **Combining be seen, be heard style with a certain wall flowerness.** Print jam exhibitionism verses clean lines understatement. Front-row fabulous meets tawdry. Timeless classics with a twist, ethical fashion mixed with highly unethical fashion. Summer separates mixed with look sharp statement pattern pieces for winter. **Know what I mean?**

Mildred was delighted and felt she could, for the first time, work (without feeling a fraud) as a counsellor. She had a new – found sense of style and also thought herself superior to pretty well everyone who might throw themselves on her mercy.

41

She resumed her work as a counsellor and employed some of the little Percies (who had been so helpful creating her new wardrobe) to serve cakes and drinks to her clients. She even began to counsel me. I didn't actually need counselling, of course (I mean, why would I? I'm a perfectly formed, rounded and grounded individual),

but it was terribly fashionable at the time and I always like to take every opportunity to talk about myself, uninterrupted whilst **eating cakes** and drinking lovely drinks.

I also felt Mildred's notes, made during our counselling sessions, would come in handy for

when someone wrote MY

life story, which they are sure to do sooner or later.

Mildred now gets gifted designer pieces that are custom made to suit her form, from all the big fashion houses and up and coming designers. She even sits front row at their catwalk shows next to me.

In truth I think we can safely say
that after all her trials and tribulations,
Mildred lived happily

(if not still a little
confusingly) ever after (well, of
course, she did, she gets to work with
me every day).

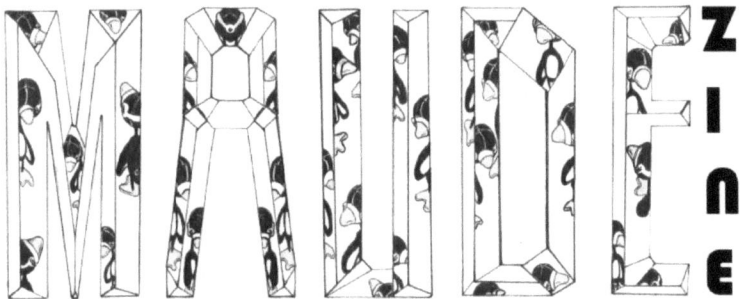

I would say I hope you enjoyed reading the tale of Mildred, but as I (Maude) have been recounting Mildred's journey it is abundantly clear that only a moron wouldn't have been fascinated, beguiled and delighted by Mildred and of course, me…

Maude xx

Maude
Editor-in-Chief
MAUDEZINE
and
Fashion Icon

MAUDEZINE, MAUDE STREET, LONDON, ENGLAND.

46

47

Written and illustrated by

David Longshaw